DATE DUE

Maine

BY ANN HEINRICHS

Content Adviser: Richard W. Judd, Ph.D., University of Maine, Department of History, Orono, Maine

Reading Adviser: Dr. Linda D. Labbo, Department of Reading Education, College of Education, The University of Georgia

COMPASS POINT BOOKS ◆ MINNEAPOLIS, MINNESOTA

Compass Point Books
3109 West 50th Street, #115
Minneapolis, MN 55410

Visit Compass Point Books on the Internet at *www.compasspointbooks.com*
or e-mail your request to *custserv@compasspointbooks.com*

On the cover: Autumn in Camden

Photographs ©: Corbis/Owaki-Kulla, cover, 1; Photo Network/Stephen Varone, 3, 28; Digital Vision, 4, 41; Photo Network/Jim Schwabel, 7; Unicorn Stock Photos/H. Schmeiser, 8, 31, 42; Jeff Greenberg/ Visuals Unlimited, 9, 21; Unicorn Stock Photos/Andre Jenny, 10, 26, 40, 43 (top), 48 (top); Unicorn Stock Photos/Dick Keen, 11; North Wind Picture Archives/N. Carter, 12, 38; North Wind Picture Archives, 13, 14, 15; Stock Montage, 16; Michael Philip Manheim/The Image Finders, 17; Photo Network/Mark Newman, 18; Photo Network/Jeff Greenberg, 19, 23; John Elk III, 22; Photo Network/ Stephen Saks, 24; Justin Verderber/Visuals Unlimited, 25; Courtesy of Maine Lobster Festival, 29; Centre Street Congregational Church/Alana Brown, 30, 47; Getty Images/Lawrence Lucier, 32, 46; Corbis/Francis G. Mayer, 33; Steve Mulligan Photography, 34, 45; Unicorn Stock Photos/Thomas H. Mitchell, 35; Unicorn Stock Photos/Jeff Greenberg, 37; Maine Historical Society/J. David Bohl Photo, 39; Robesus, Inc., 43 (state flag); One Mile Up, Inc., 43 (state seal); Robert McCaw, 44 (top and middle);Artville, 44 (bottom).

Editors: E. Russell Primm, Emily J. Dolbear, and Catherine Neitge
Photo Researcher: Marcie C. Spence
Photo Selector: Linda S. Koutris
Designer/Page Production: The Design Lab/Jaime Martens
Cartographer: XNR Productions, Inc.

Library of Congress Cataloging-in-Publication Data
Heinrichs, Ann.
  Maine / by Ann Heinrichs.
    p. cm. — (This land is your land)
 Summary: Describes the geography, history, government, people, culture, and attractions of Maine.
Includes bibliographical references and index.
  ISBN 0-7565-0347-7 (hardcover : alk. paper)
  1. Maine—Juvenile literature. [1. Maine.] I. Title.
  F19.3 .H45 2003
  974.1—dc21   2002153298

Table of Contents

NOTE: In this book, words that are defined in the glossary are in **bold** *the first time they appear in the text.*

▲ **Boats docked off Mount Desert Island**

Henry David Thoreau was a writer who loved nature. He hiked through the Maine woods in 1846. "It is a country full of evergreen trees, of mossy silver birches and watery maples," he wrote. He saw "boundless forests, and lakes, and streams, gleaming in the sun." Other writers told of Maine's "rock-bound coast" along the Atlantic Ocean.

Maine is still known for its dense forests and rocky coast. Lumber from Maine was used to build some of the East Coast's large cities during the nineteenth century. Shipbuilders used Maine's pine trees to build massive sailing ships. Even today, Maine depends on the forest and the sea. Its leading factory goods are paper products made from trees. People around the world love to eat lobster from Maine's coastal waters. Every seaside village has a fleet of fishing boats.

Mainers are known for being **hardy** and independent. Throughout history, they struggled with the **wilderness,** harsh weather, and stormy seas. Most Mainers still live in small communities and govern themselves through town meetings, just as their **ancestors** did. Now let's explore this rugged land by the sea.

Have you ever watched the sun rise? Imagine being the first person in the United States to see the morning sunrise. Just stand on West Quoddy Head in Maine. It's the easternmost

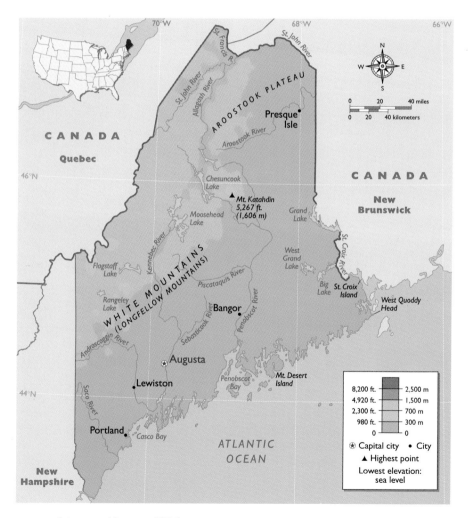

▲ **A topographic map of Maine**

point of land in the United States. Its residents are the first to greet the sun each morning.

Maine is the largest of the nation's New England states. It's located at the northeastern tip of the United States. Maine shares a border with only one state—New Hampshire. It lies west of Maine. Two **provinces** of Canada form Maine's other land borders. These are Quebec to the northwest and New Brunswick to the northeast.

Southeastern Maine faces the Atlantic Ocean. Sandy beaches line the southern coast. Farther north, rocky cliffs look out over the sea. Lighthouses rise atop several of these cliffs. Their lights and **foghorns** have guided many ships safely to shore.

▲ **West Quoddy Head Lighthouse stands on the easternmost point in the United States.**

▲ The rocky coastline along Mount Desert Island

Large bays and little **inlets** cut into Maine's jagged coastline. Thousands of islands lie offshore, too. Maine's largest island is Mount Desert Island. Many islands are just rocky mounds rising above the water.

Away from the coast, Maine's land rises much higher. Many rivers and streams rush through this region on their way to the sea. The Aroostook Plateau, in the northeast, is one of the best farming regions in New England.

The White Mountains stretch north across western Maine. They extend into neighboring New Hampshire. In Maine, these mountains are also called the Longfellow Mountains. They're named for Maine's famous poet Henry Wadsworth Longfellow. Hundreds of lakes sparkle in the high mountain valleys. The largest is Moosehead Lake.

▲ **Fall colors around Lily Bay, which is part of Moosehead Lake**

▲ Augusta is located along the Kennebec River.

Many rivers and streams flow through the state. The Saint John and Saint Croix Rivers form parts of Maine's border with New Brunswick. Augusta, the state capital, lies along the Kennebec River. Bangor, the third-largest city, is located on the Penobscot River. Other major waterways are the Androscoggin and Saco Rivers.

Forests cover most of the state. Their tall pine trees gave Maine its nickname—the Pine Tree State. Bobcats, beavers, and foxes roam through the woods. The larger animals include bears, deer, and moose—the state animal. Chirping among the branches is the little chickadee, the state bird.

Ducks, gulls, plovers, and puffins are found along the coast. Lobsters, clams, oysters, and many big fish live offshore. Porpoises and whales are often seen in the coastal waters, too.

Summers in Maine are cool. Winters, however, are long and cold. Winter snows are heaviest away from the coast. Maine's mountains are popular for skiing and other winter sports.

Maine's coast is often hidden in heavy fog. As a result many ships have wrecked against Maine's rocky coast.

▲ **Puffins live on Machias Seal Island.**

▲ A mound formed by oyster shells left by early Native Americans along the Damariscotta River

Maine was once home to thousands of Native Americans. The major groups were bands of the Wabanaki tribe. These included the Penobscot, Kennebec, and Passamaquoddy peoples. They lived by hunting, fishing, and growing corn. In the winter, several families lived together in longhouses. The Native Americans were experts at building birch-bark canoes. American Indians who lived near the water gathered oysters and clams. Today, huge mounds of their shells remain by the shore.

French explorers, including Samuel de Champlain, settled on Saint Croix Island in 1604. This was the first French settlement in North America. Canada, along with Maine, became France's Acadia **Colony.**

English settlers established the Popham Colony in 1607. It lay near the mouth of the Kennebec River. In 1622, England granted the Maine region to Sir Ferdinando Gorges and John Mason. England's Massachusetts Colony bought Maine in 1677.

England and France fought over their North American lands. Parts of present-day Maine were claimed by both countries. By 1763, the winner was Great Britain.

▲ **Frenchman Samuel de Champlain was an early explorer of Maine.**

Colonists began to resent Britain's laws and taxes. Maine's shipbuilders were especially angry. They built sturdy ships from local pine trees. However, Britain declared that Maine's largest pine trees were British property. The colonists fought for their freedom in the Revolutionary War (1775–1783). Mainers waged the war's first sea battle in 1775. They captured the British ship *Margaretta* off the coast of Machias.

▲ **British ships destroyed the city of Portland in October 1775.**

▲ Shipbuilding was an important industry for early Mainers.

Maine became the twenty-third U.S. state in 1820. Until then it had been part of Massachusetts. Fishing, logging, and shipbuilding were booming **industries** in the new state. Water-powered **mills** sprang up along the rushing rivers. Some mills sawed logs, and others wove cloth.

Like other Northerners, most people in Maine opposed slavery. Harriet Beecher Stowe of Brunswick wrote *Uncle Tom's Cabin* (1852). This novel showed even more people how cruel slavery was. Northern and Southern states fought the Civil War (1861–1865) over the issue of slavery. With the help of Maine soldiers, the North won.

After the war, Maine's industries grew fast. Cloth, leather, and paper became important products. Bath Iron Works began building steel ships during the 1880s. It's still a giant shipbuilding company today.

Maine played an important role in helping the nation during World War II (1939–1945). The state produced ships, uniforms, and leather boots. After the war, many of Maine's businesses closed. During the 1970s, Maine passed laws to protect its land, water, and air from pollution caused by the development of homes and industries.

▲ Maine author Harriet Beecher
Stowe was opposed to slavery.

▲ The USS *Maine* at Bath Iron Works

Passamaquoddy, Penobscot, and Maliseet Indians went to court in 1980. They claimed that their lands were taken illegally through treaties made during the nineteenth century. These treaties were later considered invalid. In the end, the U.S. government paid the Native Americans for their loss.

Today, Mainers face many challenges. They struggle to develop their industries while protecting the **environment.** Tourism is a growing business in the state. Visitors love Maine's quiet forests and beautiful seacoast.

▲ **Tourists visit Maine to enjoy the scenery of places such as the Acadia National Park.**

Government by the People

▲ **The state capitol is located in Augusta.**

Maine's state government works just like the national government. It is divided into three branches—legislative, executive, and judicial. These three branches make sure that no one branch gets too powerful.

Maine's legislative branch creates the state laws. It also decides how the state will spend its money. Voters elect their lawmakers to serve in Maine's legislature. It has two houses, or parts. They are the 35-member senate and the 151-member house of representatives. Both parts meet in the state capitol in Augusta.

The executive branch sees that the state's laws are carried out. Maine's governor is the head of the executive branch. Voters elect a governor every four years. The governor can serve any number of terms, but only two of these terms can be in a row.

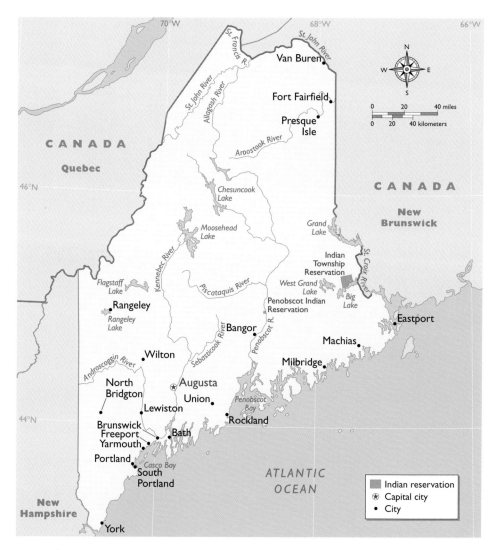

▲ **A geopolitical map of Maine**

▲ **The Franklin County Courthouse is one location where Maine judges hear cases.**

The legislature elects several other executive officers, including the attorney general, secretary of state, state treasurer, and state auditor. Like the lawmakers, these people all have offices in Augusta.

The judicial branch is made up of judges and their courts. The judges listen to cases in courtrooms. They then decide whether the law has been broken. All of Maine's judges serve a seven-year term. Maine's highest court is the supreme judicial court. The governor appoints its seven judges with the senate's approval.

Maine is divided into sixteen counties. County voters elect three commissioners. They also elect a sheriff and other county officers.

Maine has twenty-two official cities. They all have home rule. That means they may govern themselves any way they choose, as long as they don't violate any laws. Most cities elect a mayor or manager and a city council.

Besides cities, Maine has about 475 towns and plantations. These plantations are not farms, as they are in some states. They are very small communities. In most towns, the citizens hold meetings once a year. There they discuss and vote on local issues. These issues sometimes focus on police and fire protection, public schools, and parks. Plantations hold annual meetings, too. At these meetings, people elect assessors to manage day-to-day government business.

▲ **City hall in Bath**

Mainers at Work

▲ A lobsterman checking his catch in Quahog Bay

Where do most of the nation's lobsters come from? If you guessed Maine, you're right! People from all over the world eat fresh Maine lobsters. These shellfish thrive in the cold waters off the coast. The lobstermen lay their traps, also called lobster pots, on the seafloor. They come back later to haul up their catch.

Maine's waters also yield clams and fish such as cod, flounder, and perch. Rockland, on Penobscot Bay, is called the lobster capital of the world. However, fishing is a way of life all along the coast. Just look at any small coastal village. Almost every one has a cluster of fishing boats on the shore.

Milk and potatoes are Maine's leading farm products. Potatoes grow in northern Maine, especially in Aroostook County. Apples are the state's top fruit. Maine grows several types of apples.

Blueberries are another important crop. These hardy plants can survive Maine's harsh weather. Mainers grow almost all the nation's wild, or low-bush, blueberries. Farmers also produce cranberries, oats, hay, vegetables, eggs, beef cattle, and farm-raised fish.

Thousands of maple trees grow in Maine's forests. People tap them, or collect their sap. The sap is then made into maple syrup, maple sugar, and maple candy. Only Vermont produces more maple syrup than Maine.

▲ Blueberries are a major crop in Maine.

▲ **The Boise Cascade pulp mill is located in Rumford.**

Paper products are Maine's leading factory goods. Many of America's largest paper mills are in Maine. They use spruce and fir wood to make paper, cardboard, and paper pulp. Maine is also America's leading toothpick maker. In fact, toothpicks were invented in Maine!

Shipbuilding has always been an important Maine industry. Today, the state is still a top producer of ships and boats. Mainers also work in factories that process foods. Some make canned goods such as soup and beans. Others produce frozen goods such as fish and potato products. Maine also packs lobsters, blueberries, and apples for shipment to other states.

▲ The L. L. Bean Company sells kayaks and canoes, as well as clothing and sports gear.

Some Maine factories make computer chips and other electronic goods. Maine has produced leather and cloth since the 1800s. Leather products such as shoes and boots are still important products. So is wool cloth. Boots and wool make good outdoor clothing. Freeport's L. L. Bean Company is famous for its outdoor clothing and sports gear.

Service industries also play a major role in Maine's economy. Service workers are people who sell services instead of goods. They may work in hotels, banks, schools, hospitals, or repair shops. Many of Maine's service workers have jobs related to tourism.

Getting to Know Mainers

An old New England saying goes, "Use it up, wear it out, make it do, or do without." This was certainly true of Maine's early settlers. They made good use of whatever they had. This helped them survive harsh weather and hard times.

Some people say Mainers still have their ancestors' values. **Traditional** ways of life continue to be an important part of the state's **culture.** They can be seen in Maine's fishing villages and family farms.

Many Maine families have a long history in the region. They descended from English, Irish, or French-Canadian settlers. Others are German, Swedish, Italian, or of other European ancestry. About 97 out of every 100 Mainers are white. Other residents are Asian, **Hispanic,** Native American, or African-American.

In 2000, there were 1,274,923 people in Maine. Among all the states, it ranks fortieth in population. More than half of all residents live in rural areas. Those are places outside of cities and towns.

Southwestern Maine is heavily populated. However, much of the state is very lightly settled. Portland is the largest city. Next in size are Lewiston, Bangor, and South Portland. Augusta, the state capital, is only the ninth-largest city.

▲ Monhegan Island is not heavily populated.

▲ **A young Mainer celebrating the Maine Lobster Festival in Rockland**

Have you ever heard of a seafood festival? Thousands of people attend the Maine Lobster Festival in Rockland. They eat tons of fresh lobster. For clam lovers, there's the Clam Festival in Yarmouth.

Where would you go for a day at the races? In Maine, you'd head down to a lobster-fishing harbor. Lobster boat races are exciting summer events in many seaside villages.

Do you like to watch wrestling? How about wrestling in a pit full of mashed potatoes? It's a main attraction at Fort Fairfield's Potato Blossom Festival. Wilton, Union, Millbridge, and Rangeley have blueberry festivals. Machias celebrates its harvest with the Wild Blueberry Festival. One fun event is the blueberry pie-eating contest.

▲ A blueberry pie at the Machias Wild Blueberry Festival

▲ **Entries at the Great Kennebec River Whatever Race**

Augusta holds the Great Kennebec River Whatever Fes-

tival. It's a chance to enjoy music, races, fireworks, parades,

and—whatever! Bangor holds a state fair, an Octoberfest,

and the National Folk Festival.

Who is Maine's most famous writer? Some would say it's the poet Henry Wadsworth Longfellow. Many schoolchildren have memorized his poems. Edward Arlington Robinson and Edna St. Vincent Millay were famous Maine poets, too.

Some people say that Stephen King is Maine's most famous writer. Many of his scary stories have been made into movies.

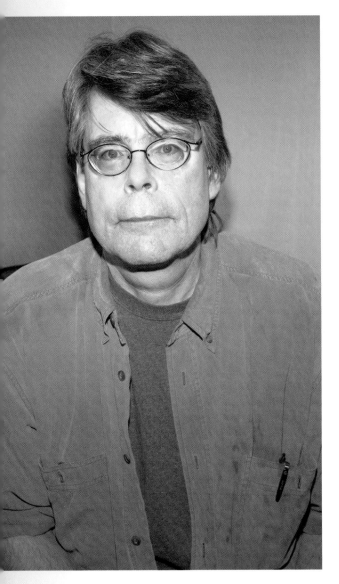

▲ **Stephen King has written many scary books.**

E. B. White is another favorite author. He lived on a farm in Maine where he wrote the children's stories *Stuart Little* (1945) and *Charlotte's Web* (1952).

Artists love to paint Maine's countryside and coast. Winslow Homer painted exciting scenes of Maine's stormy seacoast and many New England seacoast scenes. Andrew Wyeth paints pictures of Maine's people and landscapes.

▲ Winslow Homer's 1870 oil painting *High Tide* depicts swimmers along the New England coast.

More than sixty lighthouses stand along Maine's rugged coast. Lighthouse keepers faithfully tended their lights and foghorns. They guided many ships safely to shore. Now the lighthouses are run by machines. However, many tales are still told about the old days.

The Portland Head Light is Maine's oldest lighthouse. It inspired Henry Wadsworth Longfellow to write his poem "The Lighthouse." Nubble Light near York stands on a rocky island. Lighthouse keepers got supplies from a bucket that ran along a line to the mainland. One keeper even sent his son to school in the bucket!

▲ **The Cape Neddick Lighthouse, or Nubble Light, was built in 1879.**

▲ Boating on the Kennebunkport River in Kennebunkport

Many sites remain from Maine's colonial days. The Old Gaol Museum in York used to be a jail. It was in service from 1719 until 1860. Colonists met at Burnham Tavern in Machias in 1775. There they planned the capture of the *Margaretta*.

Can you tie sailors' knots? You can practice your skills at the Maine Maritime Museum in Bath. This museum is full of historic sailing exhibits. Explore the steamboat era at the Moosehead Marine Museum in Greenville. There you can hop aboard the 1914 steamboat *Katahdin*. It cruises Moosehead Lake. Another fantastic ride awaits you in Kennebunkport.

This time you'll take a trolley, or streetcar, built in 1905. It leaves from the Seashore Trolley Museum. Kennebunkport is also former president George H. W. Bush's summer home.

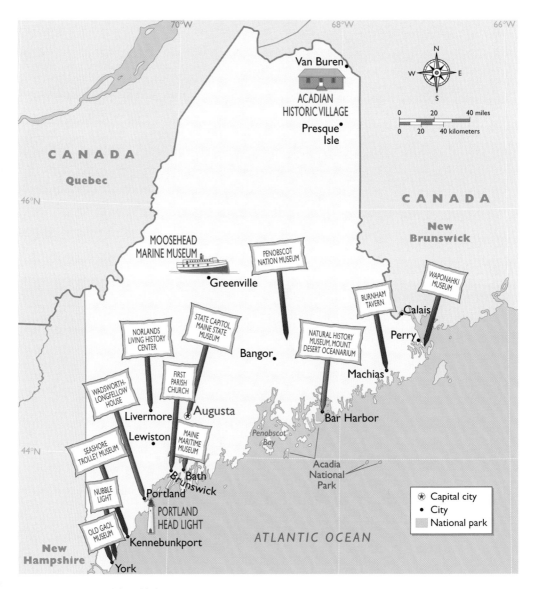

▲ Places to visit in Maine

▲ Acadian Village in the Saint John River Valley shows how Acadians lived during the 1700s.

Step into the past at the Washburn-Norlands Living History Center in Livermore to see what life was like during the 1800s. Horses, cows, sheep, pigs, and chickens live in the barn. In the one-room schoolhouse, you'll see children's desks, schoolbooks, and wooden blackboards.

Frenchmen settled on Saint Croix Island near Calais in 1604. This was the beginning of France's Acadia Colony.

Driven out by the British, some Acadians settled in Maine during the 1700s. Today, Acadian Historic Village in Van Buren gives a glimpse into the Acadians' daily lives.

The Penobscot Nation Museum is located on Indian Island. It contains Penobscot tribal clothing, birch-bark canoes, and other arts and culture exhibits. Near Perry is the Passamaquoddy Indian Reservation at Pleasant Point. Its Waponahki Museum depicts the Native Americans' culture and traditional lifestyle.

▲ **Canoes on Indian Island**

Augusta is the home of the state capitol. Nearby is the Maine State Museum. It covers twelve thousand years of history. You'll learn how Maine's earliest people hunted, worked, and lived. Exhibits about life during the 1800s surround a huge, water-powered mill. The Wadsworth-Longfellow House stands in Portland. Longfellow, the poet, lived there as a boy.

First Parish Church is located in nearby Brunswick.

▲ **Henry Wadsworth Longfellow lived in this house as a boy.**

Many famous people attended services there. One was Harriet Beecher Stowe. During a service, she imagined the death of a slave. This vision became the death of Uncle Tom in her book *Uncle Tom's Cabin*.

Acadia National Park occupies most of Mount Desert Island. Ocean waves crash on its rocky shore, and pine and spruce trees cover the hillsides. The island's coastal village of Bar Harbor is a popular vacation spot. Bar Harbor's Natural History Museum explores the region's animals and plants. The Mount Desert Oceanarium includes a lobster hatchery. There you can see baby lobsters before they are released into the ocean.

Maine is rich in history, nature, and traditions of the sea. What an adventure awaits you as you explore this beautiful state!

▲ **Shops line the streets in popular Bar Harbor.**

Important Dates

1498   John Cabot explores the coast of Maine.

1607   English settlers found the Popham Colony.

1622   Present-day Maine is granted to Sir Ferdinando Gorges and John Mason.

1641   Gorgeana (present-day York) is the first English city in the colonies.

1677   Massachusetts purchases Maine.

1775   The first sea battle of the Revolutionary War is fought off the coast of Maine.

1820   Maine becomes the twenty-third U.S. state on March 15.

1842   The Maine–Canada border is settled in the Webster-Ashburton Treaty.

1861   Hannibal Hamlin of Maine becomes vice president under President Abraham Lincoln.

1922   Edward Arlington Robinson of Maine wins the first Pulitzer Prize for poetry.

1948   Margaret Chase Smith of Maine is the first woman elected to the U.S. Senate.

1980   Edmund Muskie of Maine becomes secretary of state under President Jimmy Carter; the U.S. government agrees to pay Maine's Passamaquoddy and Penobscot Indians for their seized lands.

1989   George H. W. Bush, a summer resident of Maine, becomes the forty-first president.

1997   Maine senator William Cohen becomes secretary of defense under President Bill Clinton.

2004   Maine joins with Canada in celebrating the 400th anniversary of the French settlement on Saint Croix Island.

Glossary

ancestors—a person's grandparents, great-grandparents, and so on

colonists—people who settle a new land for their home country

colony—a territory that belongs to the country that settles it

culture—groups of people who share beliefs, customs, and a way of life

environment—natural surroundings

foghorns—loud horns that let ships know the coast's location in fog and storms

hardy—strong; able to hold up under bad conditions

Hispanic—people of Mexican, South American, and other Spanish-speaking cultures

industries—businesses or trades

inlets—narrow strips of water cutting land from a river, lake, or ocean

mills—buildings with machinery that grinds, crushes, or cuts

provinces—divisions of some countries; Canada has ten provinces

traditional—according to long-held customs

wilderness—a natural, undeveloped region

Did You Know?

★ Mainers are sometimes called Down Easters. The term originated among sailors in Boston, Massachusetts. Maine was downwind and to the east of Boston.

★ The name "Maine" is believed to have come from the word *mainland*.

★ Eastport is the easternmost city in the United States.

★ Cadillac Mountain on Mount Desert Island is the highest point along America's Atlantic coast.

★ About half the state of Maine has an average of one person for every 1 square mile (3 sq km).

★ Chester Greenwood of Farmington invented earmuffs in 1873. He was fifteen years old at the time. As an adult, he opened an earmuff factory in Farmington.

State capital: Augusta

State motto: *Dirigo* (Latin for "I direct," "I lead," or "I guide")

State nickname: Pine Tree State

Statehood: March 15, 1820; twenty-third state

Land area: 30,865 square miles (79,940 sq km); **rank:** thirty-ninth

Highest point: Mount Katahdin, 5,267 feet (1,606 m) above sea level

Lowest point: Sea level, along the coast

Highest recorded temperature: 105°F (41°C) at North Bridgton on July 10, 1911

Lowest recorded temperature: −48°F (−44°C) at Van Buren on January 19, 1925

Average January temperature: 15°F (−9°C)

Average July temperature: 67°F (19°C)

Population in 2000: 1,274,923; **rank:** fortieth

Largest cities in 2000: Portland (64,249), Lewiston (35,690), Bangor (31,473), South Portland (23,324)

Factory products: Paper products, wood products, transportation equipment

Farm products: Potatoes, milk, apples, blueberries

Mining products: Sand, gravel

Fishing products: Lobsters

State flag: Maine's state flag shows the state seal against a blue background.

State seal: The state seal shows a shield with two people beside it. One is a farmer with his scythe, or cutting tool. This stands for Maine's agriculture. A seaman and anchor represent Maine's trade and fishing industry. On the shield are a pine tree and a moose. The pine tree stands for Maine's forests, and the moose is a symbol for the state's abundant wildlife. Above the shield is the North Star. It stands for Maine's far-north location. Just under the star is a banner with the state motto, *Dirigo*.

State abbreviation: Me. (traditional); ME (postal)

State Symbols

State bird: Chickadee

State flower: White pine cone and tassel

State tree: White pine

State animal: Moose

State fish: Landlocked salmon

State cat: Maine coon cat

State herb: Wintergreen

State insect: Honeybee

State gemstone: Tourmaline

State berry: Wild blueberry

State soil: Chesuncook soil series

State fossil: *Pertica quadrifaria*

State vessel: The schooner *Bowdoin*

Making Blueberry Banana Shakes

Blueberries are a delicious Maine fruit!

Makes about twelve servings.

INGREDIENTS:

1 quart fresh or frozen blueberries

1 pound ripe bananas

3/4 cup sugar

1 quart orange juice

1/2 teaspoon cinnamon

DIRECTIONS:

Put all ingredients into a blender. Blend until smooth.

Chill for at least one hour. Pour into glasses and serve.

"State of Maine Song"

Words and music by Roger Vinton Snow

Grand State of Maine, proudly we sing
To tell your glories to the land,
To shout your praises till the echoes ring.
Should fate unkind send us to roam,
The scent of the fragrant pines,
The tang of the salty sea will call us home.

Chorus:
Oh, Pine Tree State,
Your woods, fields and hills,
Your lakes, streams and rockbound coast
Will ever fill our hearts with thrills,
And tho' we seek far and wide
Our search will be in vain
To find a fairer spot on earth
Than Maine! Maine! Maine!

Leon Leonwood Bean (1873–1967) founded the L. L. Bean company in Freeport. It sells outdoor sportswear and equipment.

Dorothea Dix (1802–1887) was a social reformer. She worked to improve life for the nation's mentally ill people and was born in Hampden.

John Ford (1895–1973) was a movie director who won six Academy Awards. Many of his movies starred actor John Wayne. Ford's movies include *Stagecoach* (1939) and *The Grapes of Wrath* (1940). He was born John Feeney in Cape Elizabeth.

Sarah Orne Jewett (1849–1909) wrote novels and short stories about small-town life in New England. She was born in Berwick.

Stephen King (1947–) is one of the world's most famous authors of horror and suspense stories. King (pictured above left) has written several novels that have been made into movies. He was born in Portland and graduated from the University of Maine.

Henry Wadsworth Longfellow (1807–1882) was a poet. His popular poems include *The Song of Hiawatha* (1855) and *The Courtship of Miles Standish* (1858). He was born in Portland and educated at Bowdoin College.

Edna St. Vincent Millay (1892–1950) was a poet. She won the Pulitzer Prize and is considered a master of the sonnet form. She was born in Rockland.

Walter Piston (1894–1976) was a music composer. He taught at Harvard and won two Pulitzer Prizes. He was born in Rockland.

Edward Arlington Robinson (1869–1935) was a well-known poet who won three Pulitzer Prizes, including the first prize for poetry. He was born in Alna.

Joan Benoit Samuelson (1958–) won the gold medal in the first women's marathon ever held at the 1984 Summer Olympic Games. She is from Freeport.

Margaret Chase Smith (1897–1995) was a U.S. representative (1940–1949) and senator (1949–1973) from Maine. She was the first woman elected to serve in the U.S. Senate.

Liv Tyler (1977–) is a movie actress. Her movies include *Stealing Beauty* (1996) and *Armageddon* (1998). She was born in Portland.

E. B. White (1899–1985) wrote books for adults and children. His beloved children's stories include *Stuart Little* (1945) and *Charlotte's Web* (1952). White was born in New York and later lived in Maine. His full name was Elwyn Brooks White.

Andrew Wyeth (1917–) is an artist who paints pictures of Maine's landscape and people. He was born in Pennsylvania and spends summers in Maine.

Want to Know More?

At the Library

Engfer, LeeAnne. *Maine*. Minneapolis: Lerner, 2002.

Gibbons, Gail. *Surrounded by Sea: Life on a New England Fishing Island*. Boston: Little, Brown, 1991.

Joseph, Paul. *Maine*. Edina, Minn.: Abdo & Daughters, 1998.

Quasha, Jennifer. *Maine Coon Cats*. New York: PowerKids Press, 2000.

Thompson, Kathleen. *Maine*. Austin, Tex.: Raintree/Steck-Vaughn, 1996.

Webster, Christine. *Maine*. Danbury, Conn.: Children's Press, 2003.

On the Web

Official Web Site of the State of Maine

http://www.state.me.us/

To learn about Maine's history, government, economy, and land

Maine Office of Tourism

http://www.visitmaine.com/home.php

To find out about Maine's events, activities, and sights

Through the Mail

Maine Office of Tourism

59 State House Station

Augusta, ME 04333

For information on travel and interesting sights in Maine

Maine Department of Economic and Community Development

59 State House Station

Augusta, ME 04333

For information on Maine's economy

Maine Historical Society

489 Congress Street

Portland, ME 04101

For information on Maine's history

On the Road

Maine State House

State and Capitol Streets

Augusta, ME 04330

207/287-2301

To visit Maine's state capitol

Index

About the Author

Ann Heinrichs grew up in Fort Smith, Arkansas, and lives in Chicago. She is the author of more than one hundred books for children and young adults on Asian, African, and U.S. history and culture. Ann has also written numerous newspaper, magazine, and encyclopedia articles. She is an award-winning martial artist, specializing in t'ai chi empty-hand and sword forms.

Ann has traveled widely throughout the United States, Africa, Asia, and the Middle East. In exploring each state for this series, she rediscovered the people, history, and resources that make this a great land, as well as the concerns we share with people around the world.